INNEN-HOF/COURTYARDS IN MARRAKECH

innen-hof in marrakesch

werner blaser

islamische geschichte als gegenwart
the living presence of islamic history

courtyards in marrakech

Birkhäuser – Publishers for Architecture
Birkhäuser – Verlag für Architektur
Basel · Boston · Berlin

This publication was kindly supported by:
Diese Publikation wurde freundlicherweise unterstützt von:

Regent Beleuchtungskörper AG, Basel, www.regent.ch

Translation from German into English: Elizabeth Schwaiger, Toronto

A CIP catalogue record for this book is available from the Library of Congress, Washington D.C., USA.

Bibliographic information published by Die Deutsche Bibliothek
Die Deutsche Bibliothek lists this publication in the Deutsche Nationalbibliografie; detailed bibliographic data is available in the internet at http://dnb.ddb.de.

This work is subject to copyright. All rights are reserved, whether the whole or part of the material is concerned, specifically the rights of translation, reprinting, re-use of illustrations, recitation, broadcasting, reproduction on microfilms or in other ways, and storage in data bases. For any kind of use, permission of the copyright owner must be obtained.

Alle Fotos von/All photographs by Werner Blaser

© 2004 Birkhäuser – Publishers for Architecture, P.O. Box 133, CH-4010 Basel, Switzerland.
   Member of Springer Science+Buisness Media
© 2004 Werner Blaser, Basel for all pictorial material
Printed on acid-free paper produced from chlorine-free pulp. TCF ∞

Layout: Werner Blaser
Litho and typography: Photolitho Sturm AG, Muttenz

Printed in Germany
ISBN 3-7643-6967-1

9 8 7 6 5 4 3 2 1   http://www.birkhauser.ch

German	Page	English
Die Oase des Hauses	6	The Oasis of the House
Welt im Haus	8	World Inside the House
Weg nach innen	9	The Path into the Interior
Innen-Hof als Paradies	10	Courtyard as Paradise
Wohnhaus mit Innenhöfen, Yangzhou (China)	12	Private house with courtyards, Yangzhou (China)
Römisches Atriumhaus, Haus der Vettier in Pompeji	13	Roman atrium house, House of the Vettii in Pompeji
Innen-Hof in Katalonien und Details der Alhambra	14	Courtyard in Catalonia and details from the Alhambra
Riads in Rabat und Fez	15	Ryads in Rabat and Fez
Grundlagen der Kultur Marokkos	16–17	Foundations of Morrocan culture
Kasbahsiedlung im Atlasgebirge	18–21	Casbah in the Atlas Mountains
Prinzipien der Baukunst	22–23	Architectural Principles
Medersa Ben Youssef, bedeutendste Koranschule des Maghreb in Marrakesch von 1565	24–36	Medersa Ben Youssef, the leading Koran school of the Maghreb in Marrakech, 1565
Details einer Arabeske	37	Details of an arabesque
Ästhetischer Aufbau	38–39	Aesthetic Structure
Museum Dar Si Said in Marrakesch, 19. Jh.	40–43	Museum Dar Si Said in Marrakech, 19th century
Dekorative Durchbildung	44–45	Decorative Articulation
Palais de la Bahia in Marrakesch, 19. Jh.	46–48	Palais de la Bahia in Marrakech, 19th century
Gasse im Souk	49	Lane in the souk
Typisches marokkanisches Haus	50	Typical Morrocan house
Ansichtsschnitte und Grundrisse typischer Innenhöfe	51	Elevations and plans of typical courtyards
Im Licht der Morgensonne	52	In the Light of the Morning Sun
Privathäuser in Marrakesch	54–57	Private residences in Marrakech
Fondation pour la culture au Maroc; Dar Bellarj in Marrakesch	58–59	Fondation pour la culture au Maroc; Dar Bellarj in Marrakech
Riad Enija in Marrakesch	60–65	Riad Enija in Marrakech
Jardin Majorelle in Marrakesch	66–69	Jardin Majorelle in Marrakech
Innen-Hof als gesteigerte Lebensqualität	70	The Courtyard – Enhanced Quality of Life
Privathaus in Marrakesch	72–77	Private residence in Marrakech
Im Labyrinth der Gassen	78	In the Labyrinth of Lanes
Haus Hans Werner Geerdts in Marrakesch	80–83	Hans Werner Geerdts House in Marrakech
Alhambra – von der Nähe des Fernen	86–91	Alhambra – The Nearness of Distance
Hinweis und Dank	94	Final Remark and Acknowledgements
Literatur	95	Bibliography
Privathaus in Marrakesch	96	Private residence in Marrakech

Die Oase des Hauses

Überdurchschnittliche Architektur mit interessanten baukünstlerischen Bezugspunkten sind die offenen Innen-Höfe im islamischen, persischen und byzantinischen Raum. Gerade für uns Zeitgenossen gewinnt diese architektonische und städtebauliche Ausformung mit hohem künstlerischem Anspruch aus einer jahrhundertealten Tradition vorbildliche Bedeutung. Der geistige Ort, die Art und Nutzung in Zusammenhang mit der poesievollen Ausdeutung des Innern sind überlieferte und heute noch gültige Prämissen von Wohnen und Leben.
Das «Hiersein» ist durch die Wand von der Außenwelt abgeschirmt und macht das Verweilen zum Genuss. Die harmonische Einfügung des Hofraums in den Baukörper des Hauses schafft Geborgenheit und Intimität. Der Innen-Hof wird zu einer klosterähnlichen Oase. Die Hofarchitektur war immer unantastbarer und respektvoller Zeitzeuge für das beschauliche Sehen wie auch für die Begegnung und das Willkommensein.
Die Inszenierung des Hofes als Solitär des Hauses mit Wasser, Vegetation und Steinpflaster bildet einen weit reichenden Exkurs in das Märchenhafte. Realistische Konturen im überschaubaren Karree vermitteln räumliche Geborgenheit. Feingliedrigkeit und Plastizität sind schon im Grundriss ablesbar und gehören zum Inventar der raumbestimmenden Elemente. Das Ideal der Hofform ist rein und anmutig. Der Hofraum als autonome Einheit ist auf wenige elementare Grundformen reduziert. Die Betonung der Materialqualität und größte künstlerische Intensität verstärken seine Gesamtwirkung. In manchen Häusern bildet er ein wahrhaft repräsentatives Bijou.

The Oasis of the House

The open courtyards in the ancient Islamic, Persian and Byzantine regions are examples of exquisite architecture with interesting architectonic points of reference. These urban and highly aesthetic architectural models from a centuries-old tradition are of particular interest to the contemporary observer. The spiritual space, the layout and use in conjunction with a poetic interpretation of the interior are traditional axioms of habitation and living that are still valid today.
The "residence" is screened from the outside world by a wall and turns lingering in the space into a pleasure. The harmonious integration of the courtyard space into the fabric of the home creates a sense of safety and intimacy. The courtyard is thus transformed into a monastic oasis. Courtyard architecture has always been an inviolable and respectful witness to contemplative seeing, to encounters and hospitality.
The staging of the courtyard as a solitary element of the house with water, vegetation and stone pavement represents a far-reaching digression into a world of fairy tales. Realistic contours in the enclosed rectangle convey a sense of spatial shelter. Detailed divisions and plasticity are evident even in the plan and are part of the inventory of space-defining elements. The ideal courtyard form is pure and graceful. Reduced to a few basic forms, the courtyard is distilled into an autonomous unit. The emphasis of material qualities and heightened artistry enhance its overall effect. In some homes, the courtyard is truly a representative bijou.

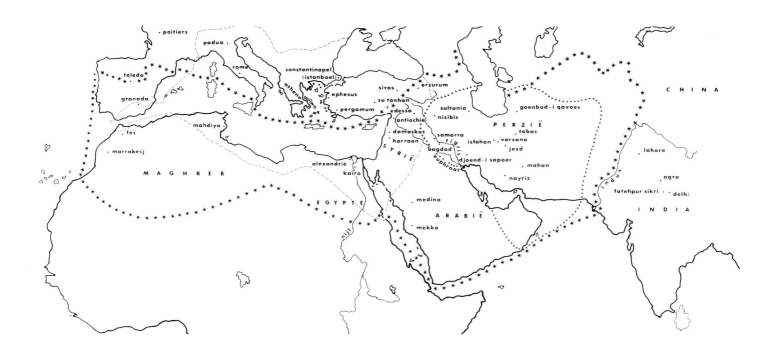

Landkarte: Islamische Kultur (Stern), Persisches Reich (Kreuz), Byzantinisches Reich (Punkte). Aus: Fred Ros u.a., Islamathematica. Rotterdam 1973
Map: Islamic culture (star), Persian Empire (cross), Byzantine Empire (dotted line). From: Fred Ros et al., Islamathematica. Rotterdam 1973

Welt im Haus

Diese Darstellung soll uns die besondere Wohnform der «Welt im Haus» nahe bringen. Sie soll dazu anregen, die stadträumlichen Qualitäten dieser tradierten Hofform wieder zu entdecken.
Die Komposition der Hofgestalt beruht auf einer lange bewährten Bauform. Diese Klassiker des Nahen und Fernen Ostens gehen auf Jahrtausende zurück – und dies ohne Verlust ihrer Ausstrahlung. In der umfassenden Kulisse der Geschichte des Islams bleibt die einheitliche Perspektive zum immer noch vorbildlichen Innen-Hof hin überzeugend. Die künstlerische Ausformung korrespondiert mit Zeichen und Symbolen des islamischen Geistes. Dies macht die bebauten Höfe zu Besonderheiten.
Der erdgeschossige Hof ist das zentrale Element im zweistöckigen Wohnhaus. Er versinnbildlicht die Analogie zum Himmel in einem von Trockenheit und Hitze geprägten Klima. Das Wasserbecken etwa in der Achse des Hofes befeuchtet die Luft und suggeriert auch durch sein plätscherndes Geräusch eine kühlende Wirkung. Die Natur im Hof erzeugt einen paradiesähnlichen Zustand von innerster Ruhe und Zufriedenheit.

World Inside the House

This image illustrates the unique living arrangement of the "domestic universe". It serves as an inspiration to rediscover the urban qualities of this traditional courtyard form.
The courtyard composition is founded in an ancient proven building form. Classic examples in the Middle and Far East date back for millennia – without losing their fascination. Against the vast background of Islamic history, the unchanging attitude toward the timeless form of the courtyard is infinitely compelling. The artistic details correspond to the signs and symbols of the Islamic spirit. This transforms the built courtyards into unique features.
The courtyard at ground level is the central element of the two-story home. It symbolizes the analogy to the sky in a climate characterized by aridity and heat. The pool centered on the axis of the courtyard, for example, humidifies the air and also signals its cooling effect with the tinkling sound of running water. The vegetation in the courtyard creates a paradisiacal state of innermost tranquility and contentedness.

Weg nach innen

Zum Lichthof in der Hausmitte gelangt man über einen dunklen, verwinkelten Gang. Es ist der Weg nach innen: vom Dunkeln ins Helle, von der Straße zur Oase, vom Lärm zur Stille, von der Höhle ins Freie. Von dort aus erschließen sich die Räume.
Der Hofraum lädt zur Ruhe und Zurückgezogenheit ein. Diesen begrenzten und stillen Frieden, diese schweigende, weiße kleine Unendlichkeit gliedert die Sonnenhelle mit Licht und Schatten. Erst durch die dunkle Flucht des Ganges kommt der intensive Einfall des Lichts in der Hofpartie zu seinem eigensten Ausdruck.
Der Himmel ist nichts anderes als die größte Tiefe unermesslichen Lichts, welches sich den Augen des Menschen als blaue Farbe entfaltet. Das Ultramarin ist edel und schön, im Islam die Königin der Farben. Die maurische Kultur ist eine «blaue» Kultur, in ihrer Symbolik und ihren Empfindungen engstens damit verbunden. Der Lichthof ist deshalb zu verstehen als Ethik des Gestaltens mit der Natur, das Schöne als etwas Vollkommenes zeigend.

The Path into the Interior

A dark, winding path leads to the atrium at the center of the house. This is the path inward: from darkness into light, from the street to the oasis, from noise to silence, from the cave into the open. All rooms open onto this space.
The courtyard is an invitation to tranquility and seclusion. This delimited and silent peace, this hushed, small white infinity is divided into light and shadow by the sun. The intensity of the light in the courtyard is only fully expressed in contrast to the dark passage of the path.
The sky is no more and no less than the greatest depth of immeasurable light, unfolding as a canopy of blue in front of the human eye. Ultramarine is noble and beautiful – the queen of colours in the Islam. The Moorish culture is a "blue" culture, its symbolism and sensibilities are always closely linked to the colour blue. The atrium should thus be understood as an ethic of designing with nature revealing beauty as perfection.

Innen-Hof als Paradies

Der typische Innen-Hof im Nahen und Fernen Osten ist eine ganzheitliche Lösung. Geschlossenheit und Offenheit sind Merkmale dieser Höfe. Sie schaffen eine helle und freundliche Atmosphäre, und sie bilden die offene Mitte des geschlossenen Wohnbereichs.
Unbepflanzte Innen-Höfe heißen im Arabischen «Dar», während diejenigen mit einem eigentlichen Garten «Riad» (Garten) genannt werden. Natur als Gestaltungselement harmonisiert dort in Form von Wasser und Bepflanzung den Innen-Hof. Der Himmel öffnet sich, eingefasst von den Hausmauern, wie ein transluzentes Gewölbe über dem Hofraum. Boden und Luftabschluss bilden die Horizontale. Die umschließenden Mauern verkörpern die Vertikale und machen den Hof zu einer von der Außenwelt abgeschlossenen Oase.
Mehr als nur ein Nutzobjekt, dient der Innen-Hof zur Begegnung und familiären Kommunikation und ergänzt somit die Innenräume. Die Hausdame kann sich in diesem Komplex voll entfalten. Die persönliche Lebenswelt kommt im Innen-Hof zum Klingen: der Farbenklang, die Reinheit des Wasserspiels, die stimmungsvoll aufeinander bezogene Visualisierung. Wohltuend ist die Privatheit dieses sparsam ausgestalteten Raumes. Er besticht durch Klarheit und Disziplin, wie ein symbolisches Destillat orientalischer Welt-Architektur. Das lichte Innere von erlesener Eleganz ist der Entfaltungsort für menschliche Beziehungen und soziale Verflechtungen, für Stimmungen und Gefühle. Äußere, hierarchische Hindernisse treten hier in den Hintergrund. Das kollektive Unbewusste beeinflusst die Anwesenden und ist gleichsam Teil dieses kulturellen Lebensraums.

Courtyard as Paradise

The typical courtyards of the Middle and Far East are based on an integrated solution. They are characterized by enclosure and openness. They create a bright and friendly ambience, and constitute the open core of the enclosed living quarters. Courtyards without vegetation are called "dar" in Arabic, while those with gardens are referred to as "ryad" (garden). As a design element, nature creates harmony in the courtyard in the form of water and vegetation.
Surrounded by the walls of the house, the sky opens like a translucent vault above the courtyard. The ground and roofline mark the horizontal boundary. The surrounding walls embody the vertical and transform the courtyard into an oasis secluded from the outside world.
More than a mere utilitarian feature, the courtyard is a meeting place and forum for family communication, thereby complementing the internal living spaces. Within this complex, the woman of the house can fully come into her own. The personal sphere comes alive in the courtyard: the array of colours, the purity of the water, the evocatively harmonized visualization. The privacy of the sparsely decorated space acts as a balm. It enchants through clarity and discipline, much like a symbolic distillate of Oriental world architecture. The sublimely elegant bright interior is the place where human relationships and social interactions unfold, a place of moods and feelings. External, hierarchical obstacles recede into the background. The collective unconscious acts upon those present and is, at the same time, a part of this cultural environment.

Innen-Hof im Fernen Osten, Yi-Pu-Anlage eines Kindergartens in Yangzhou (China)	12
Klassisches Atriumhaus der Vettier in Pompeji (Italien)	13
Typisches Patiohaus aus Katalonien und aus der Alhambra in Granada (Spanien). Details: Springbrunnen mit Wandmosaik	14
Ansicht von Riads in Rabat und in Fez (Marokko)	15

Courtyard in the Far East, Yi Pu ensemble of a kindergarden in Yangzhou (China)	12
Classic atrium: the House of the Vettii in Pompeii (Italy)	13
Typical patio house in Catalonia and on the Alhambra in Granada (Spain). Details of fountain with wall mosaic	14
View of ryads in Rabat and in Fez (Morroco)	15

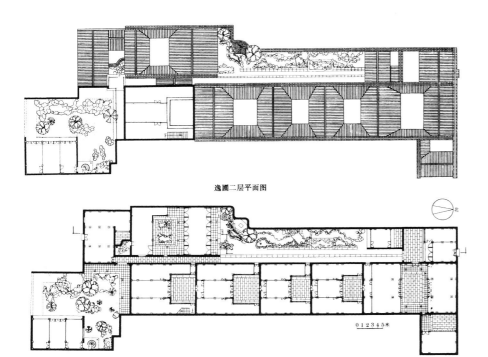

逸圃二层平面图

逸圃底层平面图

Wohnhaus mit Innenhöfen, Yangzhou (China)

Private house with courtyards, Yangzhou (China)

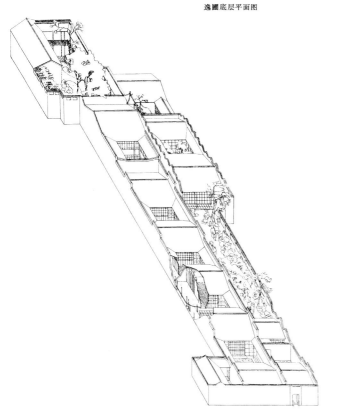

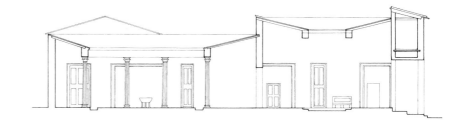

Haus der Vettier in Pompeji, Maßstab 1:300

The House of the Vettii in Pompeii, scale 1:300

1 Durchgang
  Passage
2 Vorraum
  Hall
3 Atrium
4 Seitenflügel
  Side wings
5 Peristyl
  Peristyle
6 Speisezimmer
  Dining room
7 Kleines Peristyl
  Small Peristyle
8 Speisezimmer
  Dining room
9 Schlafzimmer
  Bedroom
10 Nebenatrium
   Sideatrium
11 Küche
   Kitchen
12 Kammer
   Storeroom
13 Korridor
   Corridor
14 Nebenräume
   Subsidiary rooms

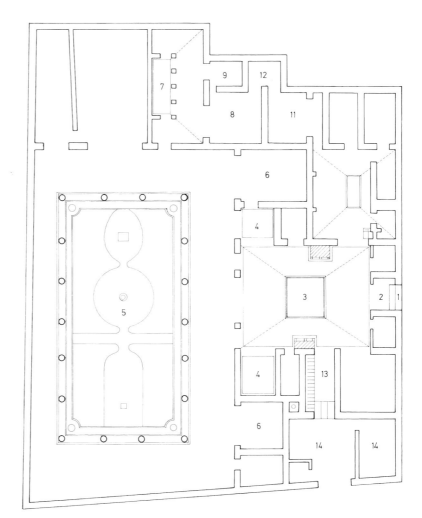

13

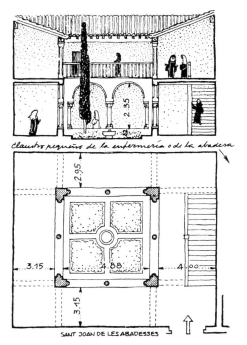
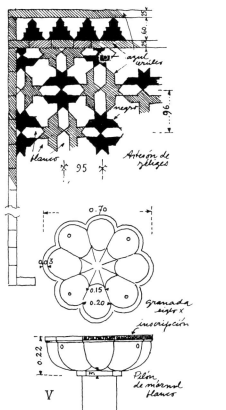

Innen-Hof in Katalonien und Details der Alhambra.
Aus: Albert Laprade, Croquis de Arquitectura 1916-58. Barcelona 1981

Courtyard in Catalonia and details from the Alhambra.
From: Albert Laprade, Croquis de Arquitectura 1916-58. Barcelona 1981

Riads in Rabat und Fez.
Aus: Albert Laprade, Croquis de Arquitectura
1916-58. Barcelona 1981

Ryads in Rabat and Fez.
From: Albert Laprade, Croquis de Arquitectura
1916-58. Barcelona 1981

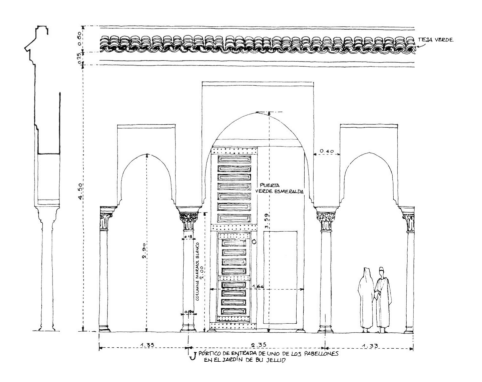

Grundlagen der Kultur Marokkos

Die Urbevölkerung Marokkos besteht aus Berbern, welche sich fast alle zum Islam bekennen. Bis auf den heutigen Tag sind weite Teile des Landes – das ganze Atlasgebirge, die weite Souss-Ebene bei Agadir und die meisten präsaharischen Regionen – fast ausschließlich von Menschen berberischer Sprache und Kultur besiedelt. Aufgrund mehrerer arabischer Einwanderungswellen seit dem 8. Jahrhundert hat sich die Bevölkerung in den anderen Regionen des Landes und insbesondere in den großen Städten hingegen unauflöslich vermischt. Seit kurzem ist diese komplexe Identität Marokkos, an der auch jüdische und mediterrane Elemente einen Anteil haben, von offizieller Seite anerkannt.
In Marokko hat sich die islamisch-maurische Kultur, die in Andalusien ihren Höhepunkt erreichte, trotz aller Einflüsse der Moderne bis heute halten können. Sie manifestiert sich in Kunst und Architektur, aber auch im alltäglichen Leben. Der Schweizer Autor und Islamwissenschaftler Titus Burckhardt, der in den 30er Jahren in Marokko lebte, formulierte dies in seinem Buch «Land am Rande der Zeit» treffend:
«Marokko hegt noch, erst in diesen Jahren gelockert, die islamisch-maurische Kultur, die eine Zeit lang in Andalusien blühte und von dort aus im hohen Maße zur Entfaltung der mittelalterlichen Kultur Europas beigetragen hatte. So kehrt man, wenn man eine marokkanische Stadt betritt, gewissermaßen in das Mittelalter der heimatlichen Geschichte zurück, mit nur der Verschiebung, dass alles Geistige dort nicht christlich, sondern islamisch gefärbt ist und von vielem, das im christlichen Abendland galt, das teils feindliche, teils anregende Gegenstück zu Tage tritt. In der arabischen Sprache heißt Marokko ‹Al-maghreb-al-aqsa›, das fernste Abendland, weil in ihm die arabische Welt ihre westlichste Grenze findet; an

Foundations of Moroccan Culture

The Berber are the indigenous people of Morocco, nearly all professing their Islamic faith. To this day, large areas of the country – the entire Atlas mountain range, the wide Souss plain near Agadir and the majority of the sub-Saharan regions – are inhabited almost exclusively by people, who speak the Berber language and live the Berber culture. Wave after wave of Arabian immigrants from the 8th century onward have led to an irrevocable mix of cultures in the other regions of the country and, in particular, in the large cities. This complex identity of Morocco, which includes Jewish and Mediterranean elements, has only recently been officially acknowledged.
In Morocco the Islamic Moorish culture, which reached its apogee in Andalusia, has survived to this day despite the influences of modernism. It is manifest in art and architecture, and also in daily life. The Swiss author and Islamicist Titus Burckhardt, who lived in Morocco in the 1930s, aptly described this phenomenon in his book "Land am Rande der Zeit":
"Morocco continues to preserve the Islamic-Moorish culture, which flourished for a long time in Andalusia and which greatly contributed to the flowering of medieval culture in Europe. Upon entering a Moroccan city we return, so to speak, to the Middle Ages of our own history with the difference that all spiritual matters are Islamic rather than Christian and that the opposites – hostile or appealing – of many truths held in the Christian Occident are manifest here. Morocco is called 'Al-maghreb-al-aqsa', the most distant Occident, in Arabian because it marks the westernmost boundary of the

seinen Rändern erreichen die letzten Karawanen ihr Ziel. Das rein arabische Beduinentum durchsickert nur noch das eigentliche Marokko, vermischt mit der halbnomadischen, unbeweglicheren Art der Berber. Es lebt aber weiter als seelische Grundlage aller arabischen Lebensformen, denn auch der arabische Städter bleibt im Herzen Nomade.» (Burckhardt 1941)

Marokko, von zwei Seiten von Meeren begrenzt, reicht von den schneebedeckten Gipfeln des Atlasgebirges bis zur unendlichen Weite der Sahara. In den fruchtbaren Gegenden Marokkos finden wir neben Kornland auch Weiden. Der Faszination der landschaftlichen Vielfalt dieses Landes steht anderseits diejenige seiner Kultur in nichts nach :

«Allen modernen Einflüssen zum Trotz trägt Marokko noch das Gesicht einer geistigen Welt, die dem aus Europa kommenden Reisenden fremd vorkommen muss, fremd und doch wieder vertraut, da sie ihn an manches erinnert, das in der eigenen Vergangenheit liegt. Gerade dieses Anders- und doch Verwandtsein macht Marokko so anziehend, das und seine Landschaft, die zu den schönsten aller um das Mittelmeer herum gelegenen gehört.»
(Burckhardt/Pfister, 1972, S.9)

Innen-Höfe als Archetypen: Lehmbauten einer Kasbahsiedlung im Hohen Atlas   18–21

Courtyards as archetypes: earth buildings in a casbah in the Atlas Mountains   18–21

Arabian world; it is at its borders that the last caravans reach their goal. Pure Bedouin culture is only found here and there in Morocco as it is today, merging with the semi-nomadic, more static Berber culture. However, it lives on as the spiritual foundation for all Arabian lifestyles, for even the urban Arabian remains a nomad at heart." (Burckhardt, 1941)

Morocco, bordered by seas on two sides, reaches from the snow-capped peaks of the Atlas Mountains to the infinite expanse of the Sahara. Its fertile regions boast grain fields and pastures. Yet the fascinating variety in the country's landscape is easily matched by that of its culture:

"Despite modern influences, Morocco still has the face of a spiritual world, which must strike the European traveler as foreign, foreign and yet familiar, because it reminds him of several aspects from his own past. It is precisely this difference and yet familiarity that makes Morocco so attractive, and its landscape belongs to the most beautiful on the Mediterranean."
(Burckhardt/Pfister, 1972, p. 9)

Prinzipien der Baukunst

Das marokkanische Haus ist eine exemplarische Auseinandersetzung mit dem traditionellen Innen-Hof. Ein Haus mit einem eher kleineren, mit Steinplatten oder Fayencearbeiten ausgelegten Hof wird «Dar» genannt. Ist der Innenhof bepflanzt und erhält er den Charakter eines Innengartens, so wird das Haus «Riad» genannt, was auf Arabisch Garten bedeutet.
Hier geht es um die Architektur aus örtlicher Tradition und ihre Auseinandersetzung mit dem offenen Lichthof. Alle Räume öffnen sich auf den zentralen Hof oder auf die umlaufende Galerie in den Obergeschossen. Die Dachterrasse, teils mit Schattenlauben überdeckt, ist ein Teil der Alltagswelt, wo sich die Familie in kühleren Jahreszeiten dem Sonnenlicht zuwendet.
Titus Burckhardt, mit dem ich mein erstes Buch «Tempel und Teehaus in Japan» herausbrachte und der sich seit seinem Aufenthalt in Fes in den Jahren 1934/35 intensiv mit der Wohnform des Vorderen Orients beschäftigte, schrieb wie folgt: «Ein marokkanisches Haus ist eine abgeschlossene Welt für sich. Der Gang, der von der äußeren Pforte kommt, bildet ein Knie, das den Einblick von der Gasse her verwehrt. Die Räume liegen meist im Geviert um den Innenhof, je eine Kammer an einer Seite, und die Fenster und maurisch gewölbten Türen sind nach innen gerichtet. Wenn das Haus mehrere Stockwerke hat, so wird der Zugang zu den oberen Kammern durch Galerien aus Zedernholz ermöglicht, die mit Pfeilern nach dem Hofe abgestützt sind. In der Hofmitte befindet sich oft ein Brunnen, eine Schale, in der sich der Himmel über dem Hofe spiegelt, oder ein Sodbrunnen. Manchmal steht daneben ein Orangenbäumchen, rührend in seiner Einsamkeit, zu der Zeit, da es gleichzeitig schon Blüten und noch Früchte trägt. Das Haus ist nicht nur eine Welt für sich, es ist ein zum

Architectural Principles

The Moroccan house is an exemplary exposition on the traditional courtyard. A house with a fairly small courtyard with stone slabs or faience is called "dar". If the courtyard is planted and assumes the character of an interior garden, the house is called "ryad", the Arabian word for garden.
This is an architecture steeped in local tradition and focused on the open atrium. All rooms open onto this central courtyard or onto the gallery that surrounds it on the upper floors. The roof patio, partly covered in shading arbours, is part of the everyday living space, where the family turns toward the sunlight in the cooler seasons.
Titus Burckhardt, with whom I published my first book "Tempel und Teehaus in Japan" and who has closely studied housing styles in the Middle East since his sojourn in Fez in 1934/35, wrote: "A Moroccan house is an enclosed world of its own. The corridor from the gate describes a bend, which blocks the view from the lane. The rooms usually form a square around the courtyard, one chamber per side, with inward-facing windows and Moorish, arched doorways. If the house is several storeys high, access to the upper rooms is provided via galleries built from cedar, supported on columns that reach up from the courtyard. The center of the courtyard is often occupied by a well or pool, or a fountain. Sometimes an orange tree stands next to the fountain, touching in its loneliness at the time when it is simultaneously flowering and still bearing fruit. The house is not only a world of its own, it is also a crystallized universe, such as is symbolized in the tales

Kristall gewordenes Weltall, wie es in den morgenländischen Sagen sinnbildlich beschrieben ist, mit seinen vier Richtungen, dem Himmel als Kuppel und dem Born in seiner Tiefe. In dem Gemach, das zum Empfang der Gäste dient, sind gewöhnlich den drei Wänden entlang, die dem Hof gegenüber liegen, niedere Polster ausgebreitet, und der Boden ist mit Teppichen bedeckt. Die Zimmer sind hoch, damit sie Kühlung gewähren. In ihrer dämmerigen Höhe lastet die Decke aus schwarzen Zedernbalken. Alles Licht kommt durch die gewölbte Pforte vom Hofe herein. Selten besitzt ein höher gelegenes Gemach Fenster nach der Außenseite des Hauses.» (Burckhardt, 1941)
Die innere Öffnung mit Arkaden bildet Außenraum und Innenraum in einem. Das Dach des Innenraumes ist das Himmelsgewölbe. Es ist, wie aus dem Koran vertraut, ein «Weltgebäude», ein umfriedetes Stück Erdenraum von paradiesischer Schönheit und innigster Ruhe. Im Zentrum des Hofes ist das Wasserbassin, das die Mitte betont. Wasser ist der Ursprung des Lebens und dient der Erhaltung und Regeneration alles Kreatürlichen. Die Wasserfläche ist ruhend, spiegelnd und lädt zur «Wohnung» des Menschen ein.

Medersa Ben Youssef, bedeutendste Koranschule des Maghreb in Marrakesch (Marokko), 1565 n. Chr.   24–36

Medersa Ben Youssef, the leading Koran school of the Maghreb in Marrakech (Morroco), 1565 A.D.   24–36

of the Orient, with its four cardinal directions, the sky as a dome and spring at its depth. The room that serves as a reception area for guests is usually lined with low cushions along the three walls facing the courtyard and covered in rugs across its entire width. The rooms are tall, to provide cooling, terminating in the dim light in black cedar-beamed ceilings. The only light falls through the arched doorway onto the courtyard. Rooms on the upper floors rarely feature windows that overlook the street." (Burckhardt, 1941)
The internal opening with arcades is simultaneously exterior and interior. The roof of the interior space is the celestial sky. It is, as described in the Koran, a "building of the universe", an enclosed piece of the earth of paradisiacal beauty and profound tranquility. The center of the courtyard is occupied by a pool, which emphasizes the middle. Water is the origin of life and is needed for the preservation and regeneration of all life. The water surface is calm, reflective and invites the visitor into the "home".

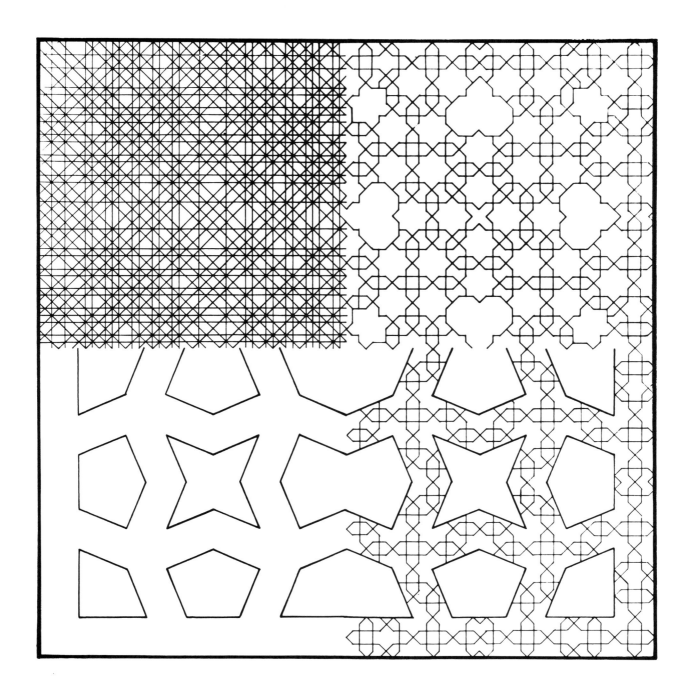

Details einer Arabeske. Aus: Fred Ros u.a., Islamathematica. Rotterdam 1973

Details of an arabesque. From: Fred Ros et al., Islamathematica. Rotterdam 1973

Ästhetischer Aufbau

Das Hofhaus bildet das Zentrum der Lebenswelt der Familie, die Grundlage der islamischen Gesellschaft ist. Vom Hof und von der Veranda aus erschließen sich die Räume. Der innerhäusliche Bereich ist traditionellerweise das Reich der Frau. Der jeweils größte und auf aufwändige Weise dekorierte Raum des Hauses, in dem Besucher empfangen wurden, war hingegen dem Hausherrn und seinen Gästen vorbehalten. Ursprünglich waren die Räume leer. Über eine Erhebung des Bodens wurden Kissen zum Sitzen und Liegen ausgebreitet. Das Essen wurde auf Kupfertabletts aufgetragen und diese auf kleine Tische gestellt. Eine flexible Nutzung der Räume ist daher gewährleistet. Die Wandnischen dienen der Unterbringung der Gegenstände des täglichen Gebrauchs. Die Innenräume sind durch eine «irdische Schwelle» vom Hof getrennt.

In einem von Trockenheit und Hitze geprägten Klima ist der Innen-Hof das zentrale Element. Er versinnbildlicht für Muslime die Vorstellung des Paradieses. Vom kleinen Brunnen in der Mitte des Hofes wird in schmalen Rinnen das fließende Wasser durch den Hof geführt. Das Geräusch des Wassers symbolisiert die höhere Quelle des Lebens. Das zarte Rascheln der Blätter der Vegetation suggeriert Geborgenheit. Die Enge des Hofes schafft einen Zustand innerer Ruhe und Zufriedenheit. Er ist auch ein Schattenspender, in dem das Licht von oben gebändigt einflutet. Der Innen-Hof ist ein Lichthof mit Kontrasten von hell und dunkel. Die Stärke des Lichtwechsels wird durch die Tages- und Jahreszeiten bestimmt. Das sich verbreitende, geführte Licht wird zum Lichtbrunnen – zur Lebensquelle des Hauses.

Aesthetic Structure

The courtyard is the center of family life, the foundation of Islamic society. The rooms are accessed from the courtyard and the balcony. The interior is the traditional sphere of the women. The largest and most elaborately decorated room of the house, where guests are received, was, however, reserved for the man of the house and his guests. These rooms were originally empty. Cushions for sitting and reclining were spread out across raised benches built into the floor. Food was carried in on copper trays and set down on small tables. This ensured a flexible use of the space. Niches set into the walls housed objects for everyday use. The interior is separated from the courtyard by an "earthly threshold."

In a climate characterized by aridity and heat, the courtyard is the central element. To Muslims, it symbolizes the idea of paradise. Water flows from the small fountain in the middle in narrow channels across the courtyard. The sound of water symbolizes the higher source of life. The gentle rustling of the leaves suggests safety and shelter. The narrowness of the courtyard creates an atmosphere of inner calm and contentedness. It also provides shade, by blocking some of the light falling from above. The interior courtyard is an atrium with contrasts of light and dark. The intensity of the contrasts is determined by the time of day and the seasons. As the light spreads from the courtyard into the interior, it becomes a light well – the source of life of the house.

Ähnlich wie beim Wohnhaus besitzt auch die Moschee und die Medersa – vergleichbar mit den europäischen Klosterschulen im Mittelalter – einen offenen Innen-Hof. In der Mitte steht der Brunnen, wo die rituellen Waschungen vollzogen werden. Um den Hof bildet sich meistens ein umschließender, gedeckter Säulengang. Der Besucher soll den Eindruck unbegrenzter Weite und die Unendlichkeit des Himmels im Intimbereich des Hofes erleben können. Im Koran heißt es, Gott habe die Himmel geschaffen, ohne dass man irgendwelche Stützen sehe.

Museum Dar Si Said in Marrakesch, 19. Jh.   40–43

Museum Dar Si Said in Marrakech, 19th century   40–43

Like the family house, the mosque and the medersa – comparable to European monastic schools in the Middle Ages – also features an open courtyard. A fountain for ritual ablutions is placed in the middle. The courtyard is usually surrounded by a colonnaded, covered arcade. The visitor is to experience an impression of the limitless breadth and infinity of the sky from within the intimate atmosphere of the courtyard. It is written in the Koran that God created the sky without any visible columns.

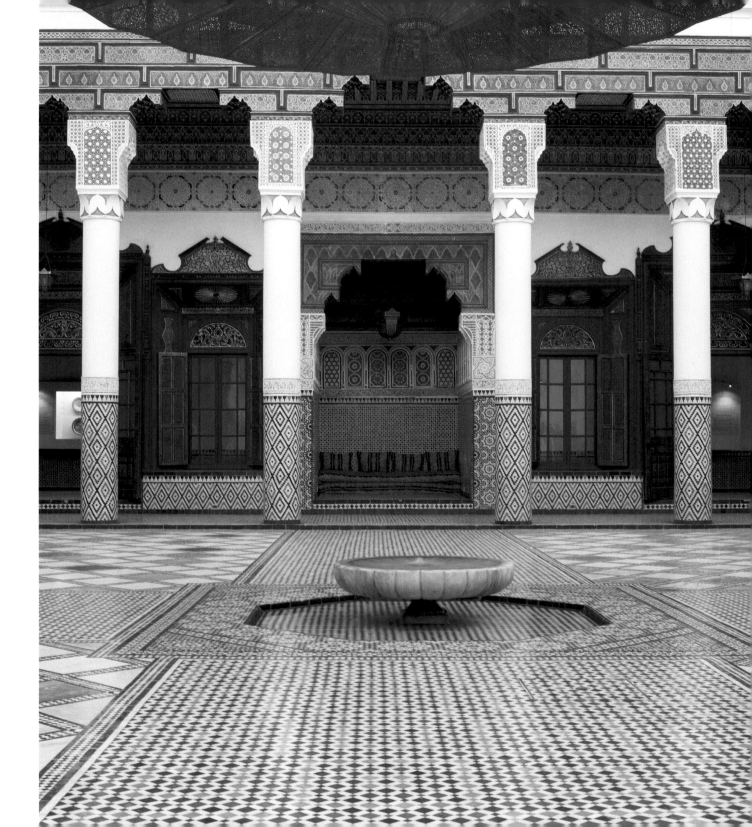

Dekorative Durchbildung

Das dekorative Moment ist das wichtigste Element der maurischen Architektur. Hauptsächlich an tragenden Teilen der Bögen und Gewölbe wurden dekorative Ausstattungen angebracht. Der maurische Stil ist nicht nur an den Hufeisenbögen, sondern auch an Tropfsteinverzierungen, den unzähligen Waben der Gipsstalaktiten, erkennbar. Die Stalaktiten bilden ein Zauberreich der Ornamente, dargestellt in Nischen, Decken, Kuppeln. Prismenartige Gebilde werden in Gips gegossen und aneinander gefügt.
Bedeutsam ist die Arabeske, eine ureigene Schöpfung islamischer Dekoration, aus rein geometrischen Formen und stark entmaterialisierten Pflanzenranken entwickelt. Arabesken symbolisieren «Signale aus dem Übersinnlichen» und haben weder Anfang noch Ende. Mit mathematischer Genauigkeit wurden Ornamente in zusammenhängende Liniensysteme über Flächenmotive entwickelt. Ein zwölf- oder sechzehneckiger Stern symbolisiert eine «geometrische Rose», die aus der Mitte entspringt und der Mitte zustrebt. Diese Figuren, in glitzernden Mustern über große Flächen verteilt, wirken wie Sterne und Kristalle. Bei keramischen Wandmosaiken, die man «Spinnweben Gottes» nannte, kommen diese geometrischen Ornamente am besten zum Ausdruck. Auch arabische Schriftzeichen als reines Ornament gehören zum Gesamtdekor eines Bauwerkes. Dabei ist zu bemerken, dass die arabische Schrift eine vollendete, unübertreffliche Schönheit besitzt.

Decorative Articulation

Decoration is the most important element in Moorish architecture, used chiefly on the load-bearing components of the arches and vaults. The Moorish style is recognizable not only by its horseshoe-shaped arches, but also by its stalactite ornamentation, the innumerable honeycombs of the gypsum stalactites. The stalactites form a magic world of ornamentation, represented in niches, on ceilings and inside domes. Prism-like pieces are cast in gypsum and assembled.
The arabesque, a unique creation in Islamic decoration, developed from purely geometric forms and abstract renditions of climbing twines, is of great importance. Arabesques symbolize "signals from the supernatural" and have neither beginning nor end. Ornamentation of continuous lines was developed with mathematical precision into area decorations. A star with twelve or sixteen points symbolizes a "geometric rose," which unfurls from the center and folds inward toward the center. These shapes, spread across large areas in scintillating patterns, appear like stars and crystals. Like the ceramic wall mosaics, which were called "spider webs of God," this geometric ornamentation is employed to the best effect. Arabian script as pure ornamentation is also part of the overall décor of the building. It should be noted that Arabian script is endowed with a perfect, unsurpassable beauty.

Der Innen-Hof im marokkanischen Wohnhaus hat die Aufgabe, den Menschen von der Außenwelt abzuschirmen. Der Innen-Hof wurde, wenn immer möglich, begrünt, und sei es nur mittels Topf- oder Kletterpflanzen. Der Riad, der Gartenhof, ist vielfach von Fruchtbäumen beschattet, Laubengänge sind mit Jasmin und Weinranken bepflanzt. Eine übersinnliche Bedeutung kommt dem Granatapfelbaum, einer weiteren Zierde des «Paradies-Hofes», zu.
Burckhardt und Pfister charakterisierten den Gartenhof mit folgenden Worten:
«Der klassische Plan des Innenhofs mit seinen im Quadrat geschlossenen Säulenhallen kann auf verschiedene Weisen zu dem eines Innengartens, eines ryad, erweitert werden, am besten aber dadurch, dass zwei sich gegenüber liegende Seiten des Hofes von Wohnkörpern mit Vorhallen abgeschlossen werden, während die beiden anderen Seiten aus langen Mauern bestehen, die manchmal von Schattengängen begleitet sind. Der Garten selbst wird von erhöhten und mit farbigen Platten belegten Pfaden durchkreuzt und hat in seiner Mitte fast immer einen Brunnen.» (Aus: Burckhardt/Pfister, 1972, S. 265.)

Palais de la Bahia in Marrakesch, 19. Jh.	46–48
Gasse im Souk	49
Palais de la Bahia in Marrakesh, 19th century	46–48
Lane in the Souk	49

The courtyard in a Moroccan home has the function of screening its occupants from the outside world. Whenever possible, the courtyard was planted, if only in the form of potted or climbing plants. The ryad, the garden courtyard, is frequently shaded by fruit-bearing trees, arbours are covered in jasmine and grapevines. The pomegranate tree, another treasure in the "paradise courtyard," is especially revered.
Burckhardt and Pfister describe the planted courtyard as follows: "The classic plan of the courtyard with its enclosed square surrounded by columns can be expanded in several ways into that of an interior garden, a ryad. This is best achieved, however, by completing two opposite sides of the courtyard with living areas preceded by a portico, while the other two sides consist of long walls, which are sometimes accompanied by arcades. The garden itself is criss-crossed by raised paths covered in colourful paving and nearly always features a well at the center." (Burckhardt/Pfister, 1972, p. 265)

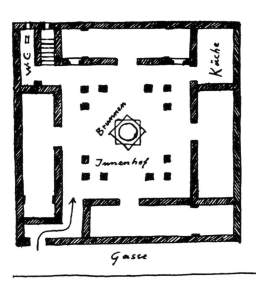

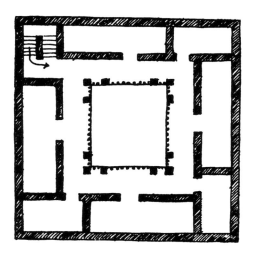

Typisches marokkanisches Haus mit Innen-Hof, Grundriss zu ebener Erde mit Brunnen und zwölf Pfeilern, die die Veranda tragen; oberes Stockwerk mit einer um den Innen-Hof herum führenden Veranda. Skizze von Titus Burckhardt. Aus: Land am Rande der Zeit

Typical Moroccan house with courtyard, ground plan with fountain and twelve columns supporting the verandah; upper floor with verandah surrounding the courtyard.
Sketch by Titus Burckhardt. From: Land am Rande der Zeit

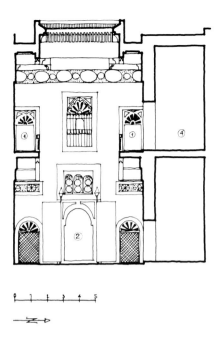
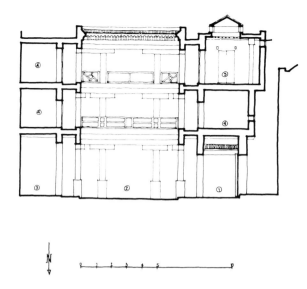

Der Kernbezug zum Innen-Hof ist ablesbar im Grundriss und Schnitt. Aus: Stefano Bianca, Architektur und Lebensform im islamischen Stadtwesen

Plan and section illustrate the central orientation toward the courtyard. From: Stefano Bianca, Architektur und Lebensform im islamischen Stadtwesen

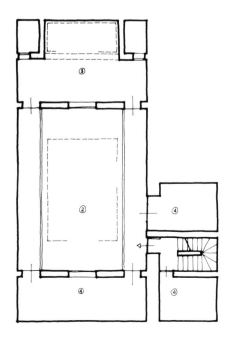
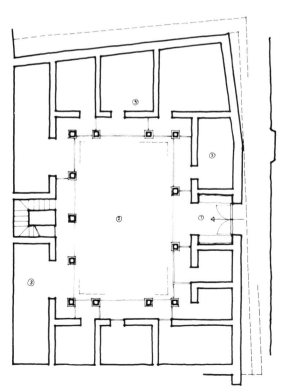

Im Licht der Morgensonne

Dem Aufbau dieses Buches liegt das Bestreben zugrunde, die Struktur und Lebensqualität des marokkanischen Hofhauses darzustellen. Von Haus zu Haus finden wir ähnliche Voraussetzungen und eine ähnliche Konzeption. Mit der Bildabfolge soll nicht nur das Wissen als solches erweitert, sondern auch auf die Inspiration der Erbauer hingewiesen werden. Das Buch möchte auch zur nützlichen Hilfe bei der individuellen Suche nach Lösungen für Wohn-Innen-Höfe werden. Garten- und Bauinteressierte können daraus vielfach Anregungen für die eigene Kreativität empfangen.
Der Beschauer wird durch die faszinierenden Innen-Höfe der marokkanischen Stadt Marrakesch geführt. Diese Innen-Höfe gehören bis in unsere Zeit zu den innovativsten und kühnsten Schöpfungen. Das berühmte Marrakesch vermittelt einen auch dem Laien verständlichen Zugang in die Geheimnisse des Innen-Hofes. Aus der Vergangenheit mag so die Inspiration kommen, einen bepflanzten Hofgarten in unsere Zeit zu transformieren. Die Einblicke in diese glanzvollen Innenhöfe können aufzeigen, wie eine immer noch lebendige Kultur aufgegriffen werden kann.
Beeindruckend sind die Innen-Höfe im Licht der Morgensonne. Das Licht fließt sinnlich über die Innenfassaden, es spiegelt sich auf der kleinen Wasserfläche des Trinkbrunnens und dringt durch verglaste Abschlüsse ins Innere. Wie eine abstrakte und zur Meditation anregende Skulptur wirkt der Innen-Hof auf die Benutzer. Harmonisch und gediegen harrt das Kunstvolle seiner Entschlüsselung. Die Linienverläufe von Natur, Ordnung und Maß durchdringen sich gegenseitig und bilden eine ausgewogene Harmonie, die auf eine geheimnisvolle Gesamtidee schließen lässt.

In the Light of the Morning Sun

This book is conceived to convey the structure and quality of life in a Moroccan courtyard house. Similar conditions and concepts are found in each of the illustrated houses. The sequence of images is not only intended to be informative, but also to provide insight into the inspiration of the architects. Moreover, this books aims to be a practical guide for those seeking individual solutions for courtyards in housing. Gardeners, landscape and building enthusiasts alike will find many ideas to spurn on their own creativity.
The reader is taken on a tour through the fascinating courtyards in the Moroccan city of Marrakech. These courtyards are among the most innovative and daring creations to date. The renowned city of Marrakech provides even the layperson with access to the secrets of the courtyard. This may prove to be a source of inspiration from the past to transpose a planted courtyard into the present day. The views into these splendid courtyards reveal a living culture that can be emulated and continued.
The courtyards are especially impressive in the morning sun. The light flows sensuously across the inner façades, is reflected in the small water surface of the drinking fountain and penetrates into the interior through the glazed enclosures. The courtyard acts upon the visitor like an abstract sculpture that invites meditation. Harmonious and pure, the artistry awaits our comprehension. The linear courses of nature, order and scale interpenetrate and combine into a profound harmony, which suggests a secret overarching idea.

Privathäuser in Marrakesch: der Hof als Stein gewordenes Symbol des irdischen Paradieses	54–57
Fondation pour la Culture au Maroc: Dar Bellarj in Marrakesch	58–59
Riad Enija in Marrakesch, Gästehaus des Schweizer Ehepaars Ursula Haldimann und Björn Conerding's	60–65
Jardin Majorelle in Marrakesch	66–69
Private residences in Marrakech: the courtyard as a symbol of earthly paradise turned to stone	54–57
Fondation pour la Culture au Maroc: Dar Bellarj in Marrakech	58–59
Riad Enija in Marrakech: guest house of the Swiss couple Ursula Haldimann and Björn Conerding's	60–65
Jardin Majorelle in Marrakech	66–69

Innen-Hof als gesteigerte Lebensqualität

Starken Persönlichkeiten gleich evozieren offene Innen-Höfe die klare Vorstellung einer gesteigerten Lebensqualität. Aus dem jeweiligen Zeitgeist entstanden, verbinden sie Gestaltung mit Natur und überraschen durch ihre vegetabile und künstlerische Anordnung. Dadurch wird jeder Innen-Hof gleichsam zum Unikat.
Seit Jahrhunderten haben die Menschen eine enge Beziehung zu dieser Hofform. Die Sehnsucht nach dem Zusammenleben mit der Natur ist ungebrochen. Die Gestalt des Gartenhofes ist begründet im Naturbezug eines bildhaft inszenierten Gartens. Die atmosphärischen Verhältnisse sind offen und strahlend. Sein Stimmungscharakter ist heiter und feierlich. Der Innen-Hof lebt vom Licht, in ihm wird der kosmische Bezug der Erde zum All angedeutet.
Der Innen-Hof hat eine Doppelnatur – er ist sowohl Innenraum als auch bewohnbarer Außenraum. Der Hof hat keinen Ausblick und keinen Horizont – allseitig geschlossen, öffnet sich nur nach oben eine Welt ohne Grenzen. Es ist der geistige Raum, der durch Licht, Helligkeit, Frische und Bestimmtheit gekennzeichnet ist. Der Raumeindruck wird durch ein Stück Unendlichkeit des Himmels geprägt. Der Mensch, dem der Ausblick in die sichtbare Welt verwehrt ist, fühlt sich nach innen gesammelt in der Umhüllung der Wände.

Courtyard as Enhanced Quality of Life

In the manner of strong personalities, open courtyards evoke an enhanced quality of life. Born from the spirit of the time, they combine design with nature and surprise us with their planted and artistic arrangement. Each courtyard is thus a unique creation.
Human beings have entered into a close relationship with the courtyard form for centuries. The yearning for living in harmony with nature is unbroken. The form of the courtyard is founded in the natural reference of a pictorial garden. The atmospheric conditions are open and radiant. Its ambience is cheerful and solemn. The life source of the courtyard is light, alluding to the cosmic connection between the earth and the universe.
The courtyard has a dual nature – it is interior space and, at the same time, inhabitable exterior space. The courtyard has no vista and no horizon – enclosed on all sides, it only opens to the top onto a world without boundaries. It is the spiritual space that is characterized by light, brightness, freshness and definition. The spatial impression is defined by a piece of infinite sky. The occupant, with no view of the outside world, feels collected within the enveloping walls.

Privathaus in Marrakesch, Renovation durch den Architekten Björn Conerding's   72–77

Private residence in Marrakech renovated by the architect Björn Conerding's   72–77

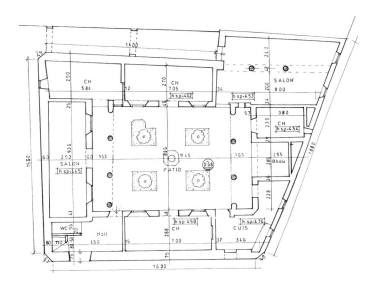

Grundriss Erdgeschoss, Obergeschoss im Maßstab 1:300

Floor plan for the ground floor, upper floor; scale 1:300

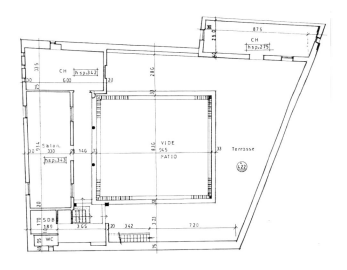

Im Labyrinth der Gassen

In der jahrhundertealten Medina von Marrakesch, in der sich seit den 90er Jahren des letzten Jahrhunderts zahlreiche Europäer und Amerikaner Häuser erworben haben, weisen die meisten Häuser schmucklose Außenwände ohne Fenster auf. Haus steht an Haus; die Kuben bilden als unzählige Zellen einen wabenartigen Stadtkörper.
Die Grundform des traditionellen marokkanischen Wohnhauses besteht immer aus einem geschlossenen Mauergeviert. Der Raumkubus wird durch den eingeprägten Hohlraum, der Mitte des Wohnhauses, und seine Öffnung zum Himmel bestimmt: «Die Fassung durch die vier aufstrebenden, mit dem Wissen und Können des islamischen Kunsthandwerks gestalteten Schauwände des Innenhofes gibt dem Eintretenden das Bewusstsein einer anderen Raumordnung, in welcher die Vorstellung der Oase, des Gartens und des Paradieses mitspielen, die der Koran mit so hoher Eindringlichkeit beschworen hat.» (Aus: Bianca, 1975.)
Diesen von außen verborgenen Bereich im Hausinnern erreicht man durch die drückende Enge des Gassennetzes zwischen emporstrebenden Mauern, wo Gassen von weniger als zwei Meter Breite zum Hauseingang führen.
Das marokkanische Wohnhaus, stets im Widerspiel zum Labyrinth der es umgebenden Gassen, Gässlein und Souks, prägt Haltung und Lebensführung der in ihm wohnenden Menschen. Von außen, von der dunklen, lärmigen Gasse herkommend, wird das helle und einladende Innere für den Bewohner und Besucher zu einem Ort des Rituals. Im lichten Innen-Hof, dem Riad, einem Garten mit Springbrunnen als Symbol des irdischen Paradieses, wird die scheinbar längst vergangene Geschichte als Gegenwart erlebt.

In the Labyrinth of Lanes

In the centuries-old medina of Marrakech, where many Europeans and American have acquired houses since the 1990s, most buildings feature plain walls without windows on the exterior. Building follows building; the volumes are innumerable cells in a honeycomb-like urban fabric.
The basic form of a traditional Moroccan home always consists of an enclosed square. The spatial cube is defined by its hollow space, the center of the house, and its opening to the sky: "The frame created by the four rising walls of the courtyard, designed with all the expertise and artistry of Islamic craftsmanship, awakens in the visitor an awareness of a different spatial order, alluding to the idea of the oasis, the garden and of paradise, which the Koran evokes in such memorable fashion." (From: Bianca, 1975)
This hidden area at the center of the home is reached from the pressing closeness between the soaring walls across a labyrinth of lanes of less than two meters in width leading to the front gate.
The Moroccan home, always contrasting with the labyrinth of the surrounding streets, lanes and souks, defines the attitudes and lifestyle of the people who inhabit it. Coming from the outside, from the dark, noisy lane, the bright and inviting interior becomes a site of ritual for the occupant and the visitor. Ancient history comes alive in the bright courtyard, the ryad, the garden with a fountain as a symbol of paradise on earth.

Haus Hans Werner Geerdts in Marrakesch; große Hohlform des Hofes als bedeutungsvolles Zentrum des Hauses   80–83

The house of Hans Werner Geerdts in Marrakech; the spaciously shaped courtyard as the center of importance of the house   80–83

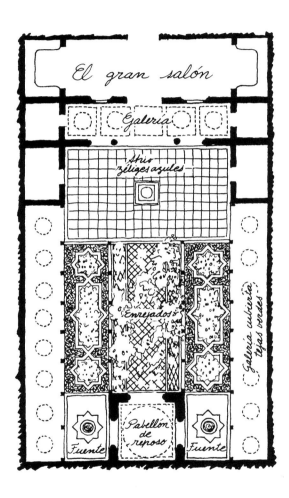

Zeichnungen, aus: Albert Laprade,
Croquis de Arquitectura 1916-58. Barcelona 1981

Drawings reproduced from: Albert Laprade,
Croquis de Arquitectura 1916-58. Barcelona 1981

Skizze von Titus Burckhardt.
Aus: Land am Rande der Zeit

Sketch by Titus Burckhardt.
From: Land am Rande der Zeit

Alhambra – von der Nähe des Fernen

In der Alhambra in Granada, im 13. und 14. Jahrhundert von den maurischen Königen der Nasriden-Dynastie erbaut, zeigt sich der Typus Innen-Hof der islamischen Welt auf prächtige Weise. Dort wird einem heute noch orientalischer Zauber in den Innen-Höfen mit ihrer Ornamentik und ihrer kunstvollen Wasser-Architektur vorgeführt. Der Einfluss der Alhambra ist meist der erste Gedanke, der den Mitteleuropäern kommt, wenn vom offenen und geschlossenen Hof gesprochen wird. Die Nähe des Fernen geht daher wie ein roter Faden durch dieses Buch und kann so für uns zum wirksamen Zeitgeist werden.

Die Folge der Fotos beginnt mit dem Hof der Myrten «Patio de los Arrayanes», es folgt der Löwen-Palast «Patio de los Leones», der seinen Namen zwölf steinernen Löwen verdankt, und die Doppelseite zeigt den Hof der Bewässerungskanäle «Patio de la Accquia» im Generalife.

Grundriss des Löwenhofes mit angrenzenden Sälen (Zustand heute)
Aus: Jules Grécy, Die Alhambra zu Granada. Worms 1990

Plan of Lion Court with adjacent columns (as it appears today)
From: Jules Grécy, Die Alhambra zu Granada. Worms 1990

Alhambra – The Nearness of Distance

In the Alhambra in Granada, built in the 13th and 14th century by the Moorish Kings of the Nasrid dynasty, the courtyard typology of the Islamic world unfolds in a glorious manner. Still today, the visitor is treated to a spectacle of Oriental magic in the courtyards with their rich ornamentation and artful water play. Many Europeans think immediately of the Alhambra, when open and closed courtyards are mentioned. The nearness of distance therefore runs like a red thread through this book and can become an effective Zeitgeist for us.

The sequence of photographs begins with the "Patio de los Arrayanes," followed by the Lion Court, the "Patio de los Leones," which owes its name to twelve stone lions, and the double spread shows the courtyard of the irrigation canals, the "Patio de la Accquia" in the Generalife.

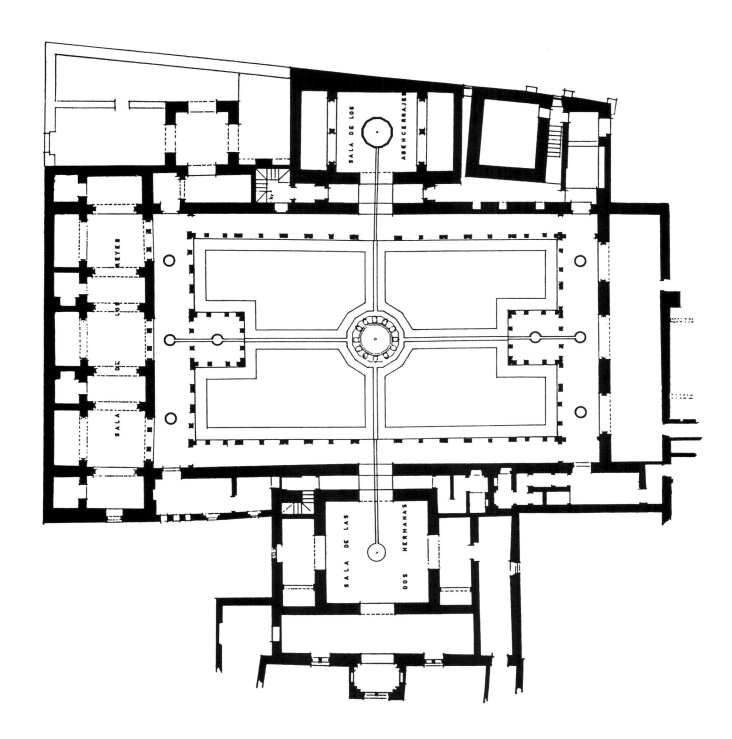

Zeichung aus Albert Laprade, Croquis de Arquitectura 1916-58. Barcelona 1981

Drawings reproduced from Albert Laprade, Croquis de Arquitectura 1916-58. Barcelona 1981

Patio con dos pisos de galerías

Riad de Si Zaieb el Meksuar

Hinweis und Dank

Die Wohnbauten von Marrakesch sind ein Ereignis des Sehens und Erlebens. Wie urtümliche Solitäre wecken diese Hofformen im Betrachter und Benutzer ein Gefühl von Permanenz und Solidität. In imposanter Weise sind diese expressiven inneren Höfe noch vor ihrem brillanten Aussehen vor allem meditativ und verkörpern Würde und Stille in einem wirkungsvollen Rahmen. Die betont farbigen und ornamentreichen Innen-Höfe sind etwas vom Schönsten und Beeindruckendsten, was es in der mediterranen Welt gibt. Eine Architektur des Einfallsreichtums, die in emotionaler Gestaltsprache ein Ganzes inszeniert.

Diese Arbeit um das offene Innere eines Hauses erwies sich für mich in jeder Hinsicht als Glücksfall. Ursula Haldimann und Björn Conerding's haben das Haus Riad Enija in Marrakesch in ein elegantes Gästehaus mit Flair für die traditionelle marokkanische Baukultur umgebaut. Mein Dank gilt dem kreativen Ehepaar in Marrakesch, das mit Liebe und Sensibilität das Hausinnere und die Gartenhöfe in ein Bijou wie aus der arabischen Erzählung «Tausendundeine Nacht» umgewandelt hat. Sie haben auch selbstlos geholfen, mir die Türen zu den anderen paradiesischen Höfen der Stadt zu öffnen. Dies alles verhalf dem Verfasser des Buches zur angemessenen inneren Imagination.

Final Remark and Acknowledgments

The homes in Marrakesh are an event of seeing and experiencing. Like primeval solitary structures, these courtyards awaken a sense of permanence and solidity in the observer and the user. Aside from their splendid appearance, these expressive courtyards are above all meditative and embody dignity and tranquility in an impressive setting. The colourful and richly ornamented courtyards are among the most beautiful and impressive sites in the Mediterranean world. An architecture of inventiveness, which stages an ensemble in an emotional visual language.

This work on the open interior of a house has proven to be a stroke of luck for me in every respect. Ursula Haldimann and Björn Conerding's have converted the Riad Enija house in Marrakech into an elegant guesthouse with a true sense for traditional Moroccan architecture. I am deeply indebted to this creative couple in Marrakech, who have transformed the interior and the courtyard gardens with love and sensitivity into a jewel taken straight out of the "Arabian Nights." They also selflessly assisted me in opening doors onto the other paradisiacal courtyard of the city. This generosity helped the author of this work to discover his own inner imagination on the subject.

Literatur / Bibliography

Bianca, Stefano	*Architektur und Lebensform im islamischen Stadtwesen.*
	Zürich: Artemis Verlag, 1975.
Blaser, Werner	*Atrium.*
	Basel: Wepf Verlag, 1985.
Burckhardt, Titus	*Land am Rande der Zeit. Eine Beschreibung der marokkanischen Kultur.*
	Basel: Urs Graf Verlag, 1941.
Burckhardt, Titus, Pfister Werner	*Marokko. Ein Reiseführer.*
	Olten: Walter Verlag, 1972.
Congzhou, Chen	*The Gardens of Yangzhou.*
	Hong Kong: Joint Publishing Co., 1983.
Grécy, Jules	*Die Alhambra zu Granada.*
	Wernersche Verlagsgesellschaft GmbH, Worms, 1990.
Laprade, Albert	*Croquis de Arquitectura 1916-58.*
	Barcelona: Editorial Gustavo Gili, 1981.
	© pour l'édition orginale en français, Editions Berger – Levrault, Paris
Ros, Fred et al.	*Islamathematica.*
	Rotterdam: Museum voor Land- en Volkenkunde, 1973.

Zeichnung auf Vorsatz: Albert Laprade. Innen-Hof in Fez.
Aus: Albert Laprade, Croquis de Architectura 1916-58. Barcelona, 1981

Drawing on endpapers: Albert Laprade. Courtyard in Fez.
From: Albert Laprade, Croquis de Architectura 1916-58. Barcelona, 1981

Alle Fotos von Werner Blaser / All photographs by Werner Blaser